A ROOKIE BIOGRAPHY

EUGENE FIELD

The Children's Poet

By Carol Greene

CHILDRENS PRESS ®

CHICAGO

This book is for
Frances Kerber Walrond,
Director of the Eugene Field House and Toy Museum,
and Charles Kellogg Field III,
grandson of Eugene Field,
with deepest thanks for their help and encouragement.

Eugene Field (1850-1895)

Library of Congress Cataloging-in-Publication Data

Greene, Carol.
    Eugene Field : the children's poet / by Carol Greene.
      p.   cm. — (A Rookie biography)
    Includes index.
    ISBN 0-516-04259-9
    1. Field, Eugene, 1850-1895—Biography—Juvenile literature. 2. Poets,
American—19th century—Biography—Juvenile literature. [1. Field,
Eugene, 1850-1895. 2. Poets, American.] I. Title. II. Series: Greene, Carol.
Rookie biography.
PS1668.G74   1994
811'.4—dc20
                                                93-42863
                                                   CIP
                                                       AC

Eugene Field was
a real person.
He lived from 1850 to 1895.
He was an important
writer for newspapers.
But he also wrote
fine poems for children.
This is his story.

TABLE OF CONTENTS

Eugene Field was born in this house in St. Louis, Missouri. Right: The room on the second floor where Eugene was born.

Chapter 1

Trying to Be Happy

Once, the tall brick house was
full of love and fun and noise.
Sometimes, in the evening,
Papa sat on the front steps
and played his violin for all
the neighborhood children.

Those were happy days.
But now they were gone.
Papa didn't play anymore and
the house stood quiet and sad.

A painted portrait
of Eugene's mother,
Frances (above), and
Frances with Eugene
when he was about
one year old.

Eugene Field was only six
and his brother, Roswell, was five
when their mother died.
Their new little sister died too.

Portrait of
Eugene's father,
Roswell Field

Papa loved his two boys,
but he was a busy lawyer.
He knew that Gene and Rosy
needed a real home.

He sent them away
from St. Louis, Missouri,
to live with Cousin Mary French
in Amherst, Massachusetts.

After their mother died, Eugene and his brother went to live in this house in Amherst, Massachusetts. Cousin Mary French (top left) took care of them.

Cousin Mary had a big house
with land around it.
She took care of the boys,
loved them, and helped them
to be happy again.

Gene liked being happy.
He didn't want to be sad anymore.
Sometimes he and his friends
put on plays in a barn.

Fairy tales made Gene happy, too.
He gobbled them up like candy.

Most of all, Gene liked animals.
They were all pets to him—
dogs, cats, birds, goats,
squirrels, and even chickens.

Gene gave the chickens funny names—
Finnikin, Minnikin, Winnikin,
Dump, Poog, and Boog.
He made up a special call
for each chicken and
each came to her own call.

Picture of Eugene Field (left) and Roswell Field,
taken when Eugene was about nine years old

When Gene was about nine,
he wrote his first poem.
It was about the family dog.
His real name was Fido,
but Gene called him Dooley.

Gene wrote the poem by
changing the words to a song.

"O had I wings like a dove I would fly
   Away from this world of fleas;
I'd fly all around Miss Emerson's yard,
   And light on Miss Emerson's trees."

Eugene's grandmother's house in Vermont

Sometimes Gene and Rosy visited
their grandmother in Vermont.
She was very strict.
The boys tried to be good there,
but it wasn't easy.
Still, Gene had happy times.

Only two things
made Gene unhappy now.
One, he was afraid of the dark.
He would *always* be
afraid of the dark.

Two, he didn't like school.
He'd rather be outdoors
with his pets and friends.
But he made school more fun
by drawing funny pictures
all over his papers.

Gene had already learned
something important.
He knew how
to make himself happy.

"The Flubdub," a drawing by Eugene Field

Above: Reverend James Tufts
ran a small school in Monson,
Massachusetts. Left: Eugene
at age 12. At this age,
his father was already
in college. But Eugene was
not such a good student.

14

Chapter 2

School Days

Gene's father went to college
when he was just 11.
He graduated when he was 15.
Gene was not like him.

When Gene was almost 15,
his family sent him
to a tiny private school
in Monson, Massachusetts.
It was run by the
Reverend James Tufts.

At a large school,
said Gene's family,
"he would be likely to get
into trouble with his love
of fun and mischief."

Gene lived with five other boys
in Mr. Tufts' home.
And he got into trouble anyway.

Gene loved pranks and tricks.
Once, he and the other boys
built a castle in the forest.
They dug a moat around it
and covered the moat with brush.
Then they sent for Mr. Tufts.

The good man came and
fell right into the moat.
But he didn't stay angry long.
"The boys were boys," he sighed.

Gene was not a good student
at Williams College either.
He stayed just eight months.

Williams College in Williamstown, Massachusetts

Left: A picture of Eugene at age 19.
Below: Knox College in Galesburg, Illinois.

Then, when Gene was 19,
his father died.
Gene went to Knox College
in Illinois, where
his new guardian taught.

The University of Missouri in Columbia as it looked in 1874

But after a year, he moved
to the University of Missouri.
Rosy was there too.

Gene failed math but
he started a school newspaper.
At last he was working at
what he did best—writing.

One day, a friend of Gene's,
Edgar Comstock, took Gene home
with him to St. Joseph, Missouri.
There Gene met Julia,
Edgar's younger sister.
She was only 14.

"She will outgrow that," said Gene.
Both he and Julia knew that
someday they'd get married.

Gene had finished school and
he and Edgar set off for Europe.
They saw the sights
and Gene bought books
and books—and more books.

Eugene (right) and some of his friends stop for a picture in Paris.

Drawing of Eugene Field

He might have been
a bad student,
but he was a great reader.
So it was after he left college
that Gene really began to learn.

Chapter 3

Newspapers and a Family

When Gene came back from Europe,
he got a good job on
a St. Louis newspaper.
But the paper had money problems.
Soon Gene left for a job
on a paper in St. Joseph.

There Gene fell in love
—with baseball.
He started a team
that was so good,
it beat every other team around.

Of course Gene
was already
in love with
Julia Comstock.
By now she
was 16, and so
they got married.

**Eugene and his wife,
Julia Comstock Field**

Gene and Julia had
eight children in all.
Two died as babies
and one as a little boy.
Gene made up funny names
for the rest of them.

The Field children included
[top left] Ruth (Sister Girl),
at the left, and Frederick (Daisy);
[bottom left] Roswell (Po);
[above, left to right] Mary (Trotty),
Melvin, and Eugene, Jr. (Pinny).

Mary was Trotty,

Eugene, Jr., was Pinny,

Frederick was Daisy,

Roswell was Po,

and Ruth was Sister Girl.

25

Julia Field with Sister Girl (right) and Po

To Gene, his family was the most
important thing in the world.
Wherever they lived,
Julia made a home full
of love and fun and noise.

It made Gene feel
like a child again himself
—a happy child.

The Field family moved often
in those early years:
from St. Joseph to St. Louis
to Kansas City to Denver.

In each place, Gene
worked for a newspaper.
In each place,
his writing got better.

By the time Gene worked
for the paper in Denver,
people across America
were reading what he wrote.

Above: Eugene as he looked
when the family lived in
Denver. Top right: The
Denver newspaper office
where Eugene worked was in
this building. Right: A
street in Denver in 1880.

Melville Stone started the Chicago *Daily News*.

Melville Stone was
one of those people.
He asked Gene to come
work for his newspaper,
the Chicago *Daily News*.
Gene could write about
anything he wanted.

State Street,
Chicago,
in 1890

That sounded good to Gene.
So once again the Fields packed up
and moved to Chicago.

The Children's Poet

Gene called his column
"Sharps and Flats."
He wrote about real people
and people he made up.
He wrote about books
and he wrote about life.
He made up jokes and poems.

Eugene wrote
funny columns
about Chicago's
rich people, who
lived in big
houses like these
on Lake Shore
Drive.

Eugene at work in his office in the old Chicago *Daily News* building.

People read what he wrote
and laughed and cried.
Later, they would call Gene
the "Father of the
Personal Newspaper Column."

But Gene wrote more
than "Sharps and Flats."
Sometimes he could hardly
stop his pen from writing.
And soon it was writing
poem after poem for children.

"The gingham dog and the calico cat
Side by side on the table sat . . ."

"Have you ever heard of the Sugar-Plum Tree?
'Tis a marvel of great renown!
It blooms on the shore of the Lollipop sea
In the garden of Shut-Eye Town . . ."

This statue of
the characters
Wynken, Blynken,
and Nod was
set up in a
Denver park
to honor
Eugene Field.

"Wynken, Blynken, and Nod one night
   Sailed off in a wooden shoe—
Sailed on a river of crystal light,
   Into a sea of dew . . ."

Poems like these soon
brought Gene a new name—
"the Children's Poet."

Often Gene drew pictures
to go with his poems.
He drew a toy soldier
and a toy dog to go with
his poem "Little Boy Blue."

Maybe Gene wrote
such good poems for chidren
because part of him
was still a child, too.

Eugene's den in his Chicago house. Reporters called it "the most wonderful room in all the city."

Eugene's toys included a soldier
who dances on a drum (top left),
acrobats (top right), and a
bird in a cage that flaps its
wings and sings (bottom left).

In his den sat many toys.
They belonged to Gene,
not to his children.

A little soldier danced
on top of a music-box drum.
Mechanical acrobats tumbled.
And a toy bird sang
as it flapped its wings.

Eugene loved his children. He played
with them and wrote them stories.

Of course, Gene had good times
with his children too.

"Dear Dady," he began a letter.
("Dady" was how little Frederick
said "Daisy"—his nickname.)
"I met the old blue bear
in the street yesterday."

"Dear Baby:

"I met the old blue bear on the street yesterday. "Hullo," said he, "where is the little rabbit?" "The little rabbit has gone to St. Louis," said I. "I dont believe it," said the old blue bear. Then the old blue bear went to tell the lion. Last night after I had gone to bed, the old blue bear, and the lion and the elephant, and the flim flam, and the catamaran came and rang the door bell. I got up and let them. "What do you want?" I asked. "We want to see whether the little rabbit has gone away," said the old blue bear. Then they looked under the

The bear, the elephant,
the lion, the flim flam,
and the catamaran were
looking for the little rabbit.
But he had gone to St. Louis.

So they all went to St. Louis too,
with a basketful of jelly cake
for the little rabbit.

"You must tell me all about it
when you come home," said Gene
at the end of the letter.

And surely Dady did.

39

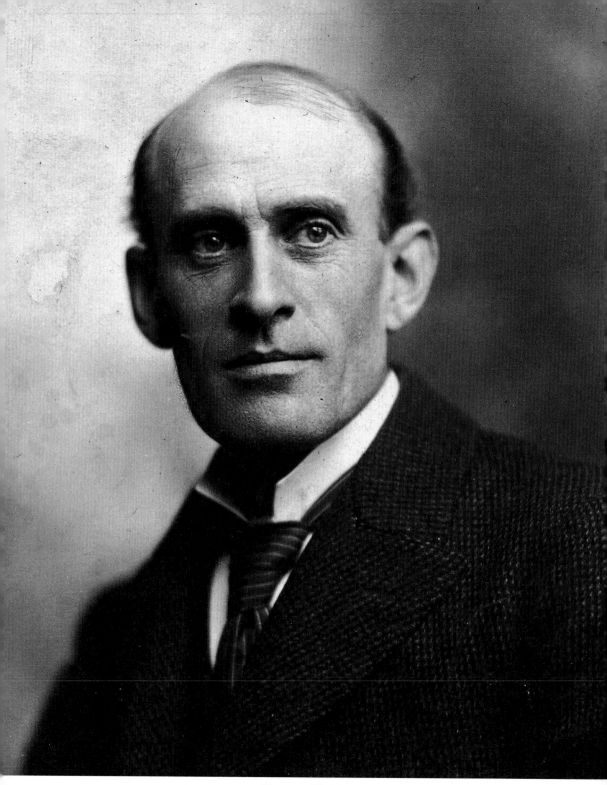

Eugene Field

Chapter 5

Gift from a Child

Gene wrote many poems,
books, and newspaper columns.
But people wanted him to
write more about himself.
These are some of
the things he wrote:

"I have a . . . collection
of books numbering 3,500."

"I am very fond of dogs,
birds, and all small pets . . ."

"I believe in churches
and schools."

"I hate wars, armies,
soldiers, guns, and fireworks."

"I believe that, if I live,
I shall do my best . . . work
when I am a grandfather . . ."

Eugene Field was working on a book at the time of his death on November 4, 1895.

Eugene Field did not
live to be a grandfather.
He had a heart attack
and died in his sleep
when he was only 45.

In 1926, Field's body was removed from Graceland Cemetery in
Chicago and buried at a church in the Chicago suburb of
Kenilworth (above). This memorial to Eugene Field (below) is
in Lincoln Park in Chicago.

Many people sent flowers for Gene's funeral. A poor little girl loved his poems and wanted to send him a rose. But she had no money.

So a rich lady gave the girl one of her roses. Eugene Field was buried holding that small yellow rose.

a sketch from life

Yet here's this youngster on my knee
    Knows all the things I used to know;
To think! I once was wise as he!
    But that was very long ago!

— Eugene Field.

Important Dates

1850   September 3—Born in St. Louis, Missouri, to Frances and Roswell M. Field

1857   Went to live with Cousin Mary Field French in Amherst, Massachusetts

1864   Went to James Tufts' school in Monson, Massachusetts

1870   Went to the University of Missouri in Columbia

1872   Traveled to Europe

1873   Married Julia Sutherland Comstock

1881   Began work at Denver *Tribune*

1883   Began "Sharps and Flats" column for Chicago *Daily News*

1895   November 4—Died in Chicago, Illinois

INDEX

Page numbers in boldface type indicate illustrations.

PHOTO CREDITS

ABOUT THE AUTHOR

Carol Greene has degrees in English literature and musicology. She has worked in international exchange programs, as an editor, and as a teacher of writing. She now lives in Webster Groves, Missouri, and writes full-time. She has published more than 100 books, including those in the Childrens Press Rookie Biographies series.

ABOUT THE ILLUSTRATOR

Of Cajun origins, Steven Gaston Dobson was born and raised in New Orleans, Louisiana. He attended art school in the city and worked as a newspaper artist on the *New Orleans Item*. After serving in the Air Force during World War II, he attended the Chicago Academy of Fine Arts in Chicago, Illinois. Before switching to commercial illustration, Mr. Dobson won the Grand Prix in portrait painting from the Palette and Chisel Club. In addition to his commercial work, Steven taught illustration at the Chicago Academy of Fine Arts and night school classes at LaGrange High School. In 1987, he moved to Englewood, Florida, where he says "I am doing something that I have wanted to do all of my 'art life,' painting interesting and historic people."